The Greatest Ten

Written by Janice Surlin
Illustrated by Rivka Krinsky

With profound gratitude to Hashem for my many blessings, this book is dedicated to my parents, whose memories are a continual blessing and inspiration, and my family and friends, whose ever-present love, encouragement and support enhance my life beyond measure.

I also wish to especially acknowledge and express my deep appreciation to Rabbi Eli Rivkin and Rabbi Jason Weiner for their kind comments and invaluable suggestions which were indispensable to bringing this book to fruition.

--JS

With immense gratitude and thanks to Hashem and to my loving and supportive family and friends.

--RK

The Greatest Ten

Text copyright © 2016 by Janice Surlin
Illustrations copyright © 2016 by Rivka Krinsky

All rights reserved. No part of this book may be reproduced or transmitted in any form or by any means, electronic or mechanical, including photocopying, recording, or by any information storage and retrieval system, without permission in writing from the publisher.

ISBN: 978-0-9981700-0-8

Published by Hummingbird Jewel Press
HJP
info@hummingbirdjewelpress.com

This is what Hashem wrote, **The Aseret HaDibrot,** After Moshe Rabeinu went up Sinai's **Mount,** He brought down these words that **count.**

I am God, I am **One**, I am God for **everyone**,
Yes, I brought you out of Egypt to be free,
So you'd know and **follow Me.**

You must have **only Me**
As your God eternally;
Never make an idol or an image of Me,
I am here
though you can't see.

2

3

When **God's** name you do say,
Any night or any day,

Think not only once,
But be **careful** and **think twice** –
Words with God's name
must be **nice**.

שומר ישראל

For six days **work** we do,
God created six days too;

4

By the seventh day God completed work and blessed **Sabbath as the day of rest.**

5

We **respect** Mom and Dad,
Makes them happy and not sad;

We must always **honor them** our whole life long... If we don't we're doing wrong.

Do not **harm anyone,**
God says this must not be done;

6

If you know a person is **doing something bad,**
Tell your teacher, Mom or Dad.

7

When you **love** someone who cares about and loves you too,

How you act is the only way for your love to show,
And be **loyal**, God says so.

It is wrong if you do
Take what doesn't belong to you...

Something could be his
or it could be theirs or hers—
Ask or pay
before it's yours.

9

PRINCIPAL

Never say things **untrue,**
We hurt others if we do;
When we talk about anyone
no matter where,
Speak the truth
it's right, it's fair.

It's okay if you like
Someone else's toys or bike;
Yes, **you** can be glad for them and be happy too
With things that **belong to you**.

Now you know what Hashem wrote, **The Aseret HaDibrot.**

These are Ten Commandments to follow every day – that's how we **live the right way!**

SUPPLEMENTARY NOTES

Shape of Tablets

According to Rabbinic tradition, the tablets were either square or rectangular, not rounded on top, and approximately 22 inches square or 22 by 11 inches.

The image of tablets with rounded tops seems to have been invented by non-Jewish artists, and while they appear in that form in paintings from the Middle Ages and Renaissance era, it is worth noting that in Michelangelo's sculpture, Moses (1513-1515), he is holding tablets with sharp corners.

Wall paintings in one of the oldest synagogues in the world, Dura-Europos Synagogue, discovered in 1932 in today's Syria and built in the 3rd century CE, depict the tablets with sharp corners.

Definitions

Hashem: One of the ways to refer to God -- Hebrew for "The Name."

Aseret HaDibrot: One of the terms for the Ten Commandments in Hebrew—means "The Ten Sayings."

Moshe Rabeinu: Hebrew for Moses Our Teacher/Rabbi.

"שמע ישראל - **Shema Yisrael**" is a declaration of faith in the One God and the oldest fixed daily prayer in Judaism. It is traditionally recited at bedtime (but also during prayer services and in the morning) and is usually the first prayer a child is taught to say.

Cover Illustration Depicts Two of Hashem's Covenants

Rainbow

And God said: "This is the sign of the covenant, which I am placing between Me and between you, and between every living soul . . . for everlasting generations. My rainbow . . . shall be for a sign of a covenant between Myself and the earth." (Genesis 9:12-13)

Mount Sinai

And [the Lord] told you His Covenant, which He commanded you to do, the Ten Commandments, and He inscribed them on two stone tablets. (Deuteronomy 4:12-13)

Tablets with Tree

The Ten Commandments are considered to embody the basic categories elaborated in the 613 Mitzvot of the Torah (Sa'adia Gaon, 10th Century Babylonian rabbi; Rashi, 11th Century French rabbi), and the Torah is "a tree of life to those who hold tight to it." (Proverbs 3:18)

THE TEN COMMANDMENTS

1. I am the Lord Your God, who brought you out of the land of Egypt, out of the house of bondage.

2. You shall have no other gods beside Me. You shall not make for yourself any graven image.

3. You shall not take the name of the Lord Your God in vain.

4. Remember the Sabbath day to keep it holy.

5. Honor your father and your mother, that your days may be long.

6. You shall not murder.
(In the Torah, murder is not just the intentional taking of another's life, but includes the intention to harm that results in murder.)

7. You shall not commit adultery.

8. You shall not steal.

9. You shall not bear false witness against your neighbor.

10. You shall not covet anything that belongs to your neighbor.

🌺 Author's Notes

Because of the vital eternal relevance of the Ten Commandments, expressed so perfectly and succinctly by Rabbi Jonathan Sacks – "Thirty-three centuries after they were first given, the Ten Commandments remain the simplest, shortest guide to creation and maintenance of a good society" – I believe we cannot start too early teaching them to children in ways that are meaningful and memorable, according to age appropriate understanding.

About the hummingbirds you see in some pictures: These tiny, exquisite, acrobatic birds (they fly up, down, sideways, forward, backwards, upside down as well as hover) are one of Hashem's many creations that I find especially delightful. Here are some fascinating facts that resonate with me and perhaps they will with you too.

> The wings of the hummingbird flap (around 80 times a second) in a figure eight pattern, the symbol of Infinity, representing Hashem's realm. As with the Jewish people, the hummingbird's size (around 3.5 inches; weighs less than a nickel) belies its courage, perseverance and resilience. And just like the tiny hummingbird, who amazingly endures thousand-mile migrations, the Jewish people, so tiny in number and representing only 0.2% of the world's population, survive and thrive. Quoting Rabbi Jonathan Sacks once again: "You do not need numbers to enlarge the spiritual and moral horizons of humankind."

So, the next time a hummingbird whizzes by, you may see it and its glimmering iridescence in a different light, as did one of the early European settlers in North America, William Wood, who in 1634 described "[t]he Humbird [as] one of the wonders of the Countrey . . . For colour she is as glorious as the Raine-bow."

🌺 About the Author

Janice Surlin was born in Buffalo, New York, but grew up in Illinois. She retained and values her solid Midwestern roots after being transplanted to Los Angeles, where she currently lives, writes, pursues lifelong learning and treasures time spent with family and friends.

🌺 About the Illustrator

Rivka (Siegel) Krinsky is an artist and illustrator. She studied Fine Art at Stern College in New York and Bezalel Academy in Jerusalem. She lives in Los Angeles with her husband and energetic toddler.